W9-CFQ-339

Understanding and Caring for Your Pet

Aquarium

Aquarium

Written by
Lance Jepson MA VetMB CBiol MSB MRCVS

Mason Crest
450 Parkway Drive, Suite D
Broomall, PA 19008
www.masoncrest.com
Developed and produced by Mason Crest

© 2017 by Mason Crest, an imprint of National Highlights, Inc.
All rights reserved. No part of this publication may be reproduced or
transmitted in any form or by any means, electronic or mechanical,
including photocopying, recording, taping, or any information storage
and retrieval system, without permission from the publisher.

Printed and bound in the United States of America.

First printing
9 8 7 6 5 4 3 2 1

Series ISBN: 978-1-4222-3691-8
ISBN: 978-1-4222-3692-5
ebook ISBN: 978-1-4222-8084-3

Every reasonable care has been taken in the compilation of this publication.
The Publisher and Author cannot accept liability for any loss, damage, injury, or
death resulting from the keeping of fish by user(s) of this publication, or from the
use of any materials, equipment, methods, or information recommended in this
publication or from any errors or omissions that may be found in the text of this
publication or that may occur at a future date, except as expressly provided by law.
No animals were harmed in the making of this book.

Words in bold are explained in the glossary on page 127.

QR CODES AND LINKS TO THIRD PARTY CONTENT

You may gain access to certain third party content ("Third Party Sites") by scanning
and using the QR Codes that appear in this publication (the "QR Codes"). We do
not operate or control in any respect any information, products or services on such
Third Party Sites linked to by us via the QR Codes included in this publication, and
we assume no responsibility for any materials you may access using the QR Codes.
Your use of the QR Codes may be subject to terms, limitations, or restrictions set
forth in the applicable terms of use or otherwise established by the owners of the
Third Party Sites. Our linking to such Third Party Sites via the QR Codes does not
imply an endorsement or sponsorship of such Third Party Sites, or the information,
products or services offered on or through the Third Party Sites, nor does it imply
an endorsement or sponsorship of this publication by the owners of such Third
Party Sites.

3 1907 00373 4240

Understanding and Caring for Your Pet

Aquarium
Cats
Dog Training
Ferrets
Gerbils
Goldfish

Guinea Pigs
Hamsters
Kittens
Parakeets
Puppies
Rabbits

Educational Videos: Readers can view videos by scanning our QR codes, providing them with additional educational content to supplement the text. Examples include news coverage, moments in history, speeches, iconic moments, and much more!

Words to Understand: These words with their easy-to-understand definitions will increase the reader's understanding of the text, while building vocabulary skills.

Contents

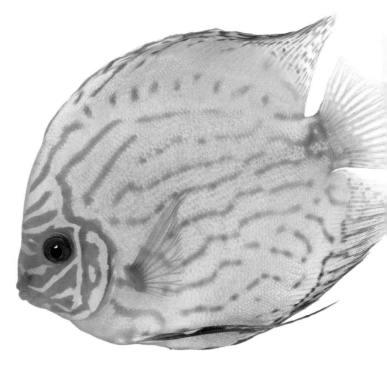

The Aquarium

Keeping an aquarium, or fish tank, can be a fascinating pastime. Watching healthy fish going about their business in their apparently weightless world is a relaxing experience, and following their day-to-day lives can be more addictive than television.

When it is done properly, fish keeping also teaches you hands-on practical skills of animal care, an empathy for animals, and a direct awareness of other lands and ecosystems. You can literally bring a piece of the mighty Amazon River into your own living room.

Fish are living creatures, and when we decide to setup and keep an aquarium, we must repay their beauty and their fascinating behaviors with care and respect. This book will show you how.

A mixed school of rainbowfish is a joy to watch.

Your New Aquarium

Establishing a successful aquarium is more like a marathon than a sprint. A truly successful aquarium takes time to establish because it is a living ecosystem, a complex environment that relies heavily on two types of organisms for its continued health.

One group is the bacterial colonies that we need to establish in the filtration systems to remove biological fish waste, and the other is YOU. As the owner, you need to feed, check temperatures, maintain equipment, and do regular partial water changes to keep the aquarium and its inhabitants in top condition.

Deciding on Your Aquarium

Most people starting this hobby will have an idea in their mind about what kind of aquarium they want. Here are some of your choices:

- **Tropical** community.

- **Temperate** community. Many "tropical" fish are actually happier at room temperatures between around 61– 72°F (16 to 22°C). Such fish often originate from countries on either side of the Tropics of Cancer and Capricorn, or are found at higher elevations, where temperatures are cooler.

A look at types of aquariums

A discus (Symphysodon sp) is a stunning fish for a single-species aquarium.

- Single or limited species. This can be for a single individual fish to be kept as a pet, or for a **school** or breeding group of a single species. This can take a great deal of self-restraint but can be very rewarding!

- Small aquariums. At their best these can be small, stylish **focal points** that have integral filtration and lighting units. Their water volume is only a few gallons, which means that temperature and water quality can be unstable and changes rapid. However, if **aquascaped** appropriately and stocked with small fish or **invertebrates**, they can be fascinating table-top works of art.

- Community tank. Take the time to decide what you want from an aquarium. Most people choose a community aquarium of tropical freshwater fish. This gives the widest choice possible of potential species About 25 gallons (95 liters) is the minimum size minimum volume for such an aquarium.

A group of goldfish requires a large and well maintained aquarium and the pay-off? An eye catching display!

Types of Aquariums

As a general rule, the bigger the aquarium, the better. Larger water volumes have more stable temperatures and water quality, and you can put more fish in them! However, large aquariums are more expensive and can be extremely heavy. Water is very heavy, and by the time gravel, plants, and decorations are factored in, a 30-gallon (120-l) aquarium could easily weigh some 286 pounds (130).

What kind of aquarium is for you?

The small aquariums pictured here are big enough only for one or two small goldfish, or a single paradise fish.

Make sure the furniture you plan to put your aquarium on is strong enough to hold it. For larger fish tanks the flooring should be checked to ensure that it can bear the weight. Ideally, always place your aquarium on a commercially-made aquarium stand (such as the one in the picture). These are designed to accommodate the weight of the aquarium and everything in it.

Another consideration is whether the aquarium is glass or acrylic. Glass tanks are heavier, scratch resistant, and usually rectangular. Acrylic tanks can be moulded to a variety of shapes, including spheres. They are lighter, but are more susceptible to being scratched. This is especially important when cleaning **algae** off the inside surfaces, as some cleaners will scour in tiny abrasions that can reduce transparency.

The different types of tanks available offer a variety of possible fish-keeping experiences.
For example:

Standard rectangular tanks

These are the best tanks that offer flexibility in sizes available, which species that can be kept in them, plus varied lighting and filtration options. Many lighting and filtration systems built in that are either hidden or designed to look sharp and streamlined. Surface area (how much of the surface of the water comes in contact with the air) is vital, as this is where oxygenation of the water occurs. A tall aquarium will have a smaller surface area than a shallower tank of the same dimensions, and therefore holds less fish.

Nanoaquariums

These are small aquariums that hold a very small volume of water. The best of these have built-in filtration units, and some have built-in lighting as well

Acrylic bowls with built-in filtration units

These are stylish and modern looking. The curved surfaces can alter the viewing experience and cleaning can be tricky, but there is a range of products designed to help with the maintenance of such bowls. The water volume can be small compared to traditional aquariums.

Themed aquariums

These aquariums are often marketed as beginner set-ups and are usually targeted towards children. Typically they are small acrylic aquariums that are brightly colored and often have themes that appeal to children, such as cartoon characters. Such aquariums have the same intrinsic problems as nanoaquariums and, even though they are usually supplied with small power-filters, maintaining suitable water conditions can be challenging even in experienced hands. These aquariums are not ideal for the long-term care of goldfish; a single male paradise fish (Macropodus opercularis) makes a much more suitable pet. The paradise fish is happy at room temperatures and is a fish that can be trained to jump for its food!

Checklist

Once you have chosen your aquarium, here is a basic checklist of items you need to buy:

[✓]   Pet Friendly: Aquarium Book

[✓]   Aquarium

[✓]   **Substrate**

[✓]   Background

[✓]   Filter

[✓]   Air pump, air tubing, and air stone (optional)

[✓]   Heater (for tropical aquariums)

[✓]   Filter maturation product

[✓]   Lighting

[✓]   Timer

[✓]   Water conditioner

[✓]   Bucket (preferably food grade) for water changes

[✓]   Flexible tubing for **siphoning**

[✓]   Thermometer

[✓]   Net

[✓]   Water testing kit

[✓]   Ornaments

[✓]   Fish food

[✓]   Notebook

Substrate

The substrate is what you place on the bottom of the aquarium. Typically this is a gravel of some type, but aquarium sand is also suitable. Do not use builders' sand, as this can be quite sharp, or beach sand because of the high salt content. Coral sand is really only suitable for saltwater tanks.

The substrate helps the fish to orient correctly; fish in bare aquariums will often swim at odd angles. It also provides something for foraging fish such as corydoras catfish to root around in. What you choose for a substrate is entirely up to you, and most aquarium stores will stock a range of fish-safe substrates. If you want a natural appearance to your aquarium, consider using natural gravel which, with its muted tones and rounded shapes, will give a neutral backdrop to your fish. Alternatively, you can choose a bright color—often garishly so. Generally fish look better against black, dark, or natural tones, as this encourages them to display their brightest colors. The lighter the substrate color, the paler the fish will become as it attempts to blend in.

Fish look better against the more muted tones of natural gravel, opposite, but if you want red, the choice is yours!

Background

It is usually best to use a background. Typically, these are mounted on the outside of the back panel of your tank. As with substrates, they help the fish orient and create a backdrop against which your aquascaping and your fish can be viewed. It will also hide any wires and plumbing hanging behind the back panel. As with substrates, what you choose is entirely up to you. A plain black background often works best; blue can work, but does not look as natural with freshwater aquariums as it does with saltwater tanks.

Photographic backgrounds are also available with underwater scenes—usually plants and rocks, but occasionally ruined cities or even cartoon-like fish. The main downside with scenic backgrounds is that any algae, scratches or imperfections on the back panel will immediate destroy any illusion or perspective of depth.

As an alternative, there are molded backgrounds that can be attached to the inside of the aquarium. These usually depict realistic rock and root formations, and can provide a dramatic backdrop to your aquascaping.

A variety of plain and photographic backgrounds are available to suit all tastes.

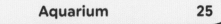

Heater

If you are planning to keep tropical fish, you will need an aquarium heater. These are thermostatically controlled and are usually preset to around 77°F (25°C), but can be adjusted.

If you are keeping large, robust fish, such as Central American cichlids or oscars (Astronotus occellatus) then a heater guard is necessary. The package will usually list what wattage of heater you need for aquariums of different sizes. If you have a large aquarium, consider installing two smaller heaters. This way, if one fails, the other will at least stop the water temperature from dropping too low; also if the thermostat sticks on one (a rare event), then this rogue heater is unlikely to cook your fish.

You will also need a thermometer to check that your heater is functioning properly. There are usually three types available:

Select your heater according to the volume of your aquarium .

- Glass thermometers, suspended from a suction cup inside the tank and contain dyed alcohol.

- Colorometric LCD thermometers are stuck permanently in one place on the outside of the aquarium.

- Digital thermometers are positioned inside the aquarium, or outside with a probe placed into the water.

Lighting

Many starter aquariums come with lighting units already installed. Usually these lights are fluorescent tubes that can be either normal T-8s or the brighter, more energy efficient T-5s. LED lights are very economical on power and have much longer life-spans than fluorescent tubes.

LED lights are very economical too and have much longer life-spans than fluorescent tubes. There are some novelty LED lights in different colors that can be used submerged. If you choose to use these to make an underwater lighting display, please remember that fish do not have eyelids and may be stressed by lights shining directly into their eyes, rather than from above as would be the case in nature.

Fish need a period of darkness, so aim to have the lights on for no more than 12 to 14 hours per day. Placing the lighting on a timer is ideal, as this keeps the day-night cycle constant.

Avoid placing your aquarium in direct sunlight. This can cause excessive algal growth in the aquarium and pronounced temperature swings.

A range of lighting is available for aquariums..

Filters and Filtration

You cannot keep fish healthy without good water quality, and you cannot keep good water quality without filtration. Your filter, and how you look after it, is the key to a successful aquarium. It is the main life-support mechanism in your fish tank, functioning as a mini-sewerage plant by facilitating the nitrogen cycle.

Filtration can be divided into three main types, and most modern filters do all three.

1. Physical filtration

Physical filtration usually involves drawing water through a fine mesh synthetic polymer substance (filter media) that traps any suspended particles such as faeces or plant debris. This will physically clean the water.

2. Biological filtration

Fortunately, all the beneficial bacteria important in the nitrogen cycle like the same conditions—plenty of food, plenty of oxygen, tropical temperatures, and a suitable place to live. By using certain material, such as highly porous minerals, ceramics, or sponges, which have a huge surface area relative to their volume, and placing these in a good water flow, we can provide the optimum conditions for these beneficial bacteria that will help break down harmful chemicals into harmless ones.

Establishing enough of these beneficial bacteria to support a healthy fish community is often referred to as cycling or maturing your aquarium.

Chemical filtration

At one time the only real chemical filtration available to fish keepers was activated charcoal. This has special properties that help it absorb a wide variety of dissolved compounds—good and bad—from the water. Activated charcoal can remove the organic products that naturally dye water a yellowish color and so helps to improve clarity. Activated charcoal is now available coated onto sponges for insertion into internal power-filters.

Other forms of chemical filtration have become available recently, including products that will remove dissolved phosphates and even nitrates, both of which can be a cause of nuisance algae.

Filter media

1. Aqua Carbon

2. Filter Wool

3. Nitrex

4. Bio-media

Corydoras sterbai

What Fishkeepers Need to Know About Water

Aquarists like to keep fish. Fish live in water, so aquarists need to know about water. Obvious, isn't it? Here are the basics of what you need to know.

Now let's get the first misconception out of the way—clear water is not always good water. Clear water can be good water, but so can pea-soup green water packed with suspended algae. Clear water can be bad water if it has high levels of ammonia in it. You cannot tell just by looking. It is the quality of the water that counts and much of the expense and equipment involved with fishkeeping is concerned with maintaining optimal water quality.

To keep a tropical freshwater aquarium looking its best, you need to know about temperature, pH, hardness, ammonia, nitrites, nitrates, oxygen, carbon dioxide and chlorine. Fortunately, you don't need a PhD in chemistry to understand these.

Platies (Xiphophorus maculatus) are hardy and popular aquarium fish.

Temperature

Fish cannot produce their own body heat, but even if they could, most of it would be immediately lost to the surrounding water. Fish are suited to the conditions in which they evolved and have little ability to adapt. For example, Siamese fighting fish (Betta splendens) come from Southeast Asia, inhabiting shallow pools and paddy fields, where temperatures can soar.

t is not surprising that they are happiest between 77—86°F (25—30°C). The closely-related paradise fish is found in more northerly countries such as southern China and Taiwan, and so is happier in more temperate waters of 64—71°F (18—22°C). Keeping paradise fish in a warmer aquarium often enhances their aggression, because they are at the top end of their temperature range, at levels that stimulate breeding and therefore territoriality. Keep a fish too cold and its ability to digest food, fend off infection, or even just live will be severely affected.

Points to remember :

- Research the temperature needs of your fish. They may not be able to adapt to cooler or warmer temperatures.

- Ammonia is more toxic at higher temperatures.

- At very high or low temperatures, biological filtration may not work properly.

- Warmer water holds less oxygen.

- Temperature-related water quality issues involve ammonia, nitrite, and oxygen.

pH

The pH is a measure of how acidic or alkaline a substance is. It is measured along a scale of 1.0 (most acidic) to 14.0 (most alkaline), with pure water a neutral 7.0. Just like temperatures, the pH needs of fish reflect their waters of origin. For example, Rift Lake fish such as Malawi cichlids need a higher pH of around 8.0 to 8.1 while some Amazonian fish such as discus (Symphysodon spp) need low pH water of between 6.0 to 7.0.

Points to remember :

- Most ornamental fish available are adapted to a pH between 6.5 and 7.5.

- A change of 1 unit on the pH scale is actually a 10-fold change in the acidity of the water. Therefore, a fish transferred from water of pH 7.0 to pH 6.0 experiences a 10-fold fall in acidity. You should always make changes gradually to accommodate this.

- Ammonia becomes more toxic at a higher pH.

- It is normal for the pH in an aquarium to fall over time. The right number of fish, filter maintenance, and water changes will reduce this effect and most fish will tolerate this gradual reduction well. However, you should be very careful about using pH adjusters—as their effect is temporary and pH falls are best addressed by looking at what the underlying problems are.

- pH-related water quality issues involve carbonate hardness, ammonia, nitrite, and carbon dioxide. Your plants may also be contributors.

Hardness

Hardness is a measure of the total dissolved mineral salt content of water. If a sample of water has a very high level of dissolved minerals, it is classed as hard, while soft water has little dissolved mineral content.

J ust to make life slightly more complex, hardness consists of two parts—general hardness (or dH) and the carbonate (or temporary) hardness (kH).

A range of minerals contribute to water hardness, but the one found in greatest concentrations is calcium carbonate. Because of this, hardness usually refers to the calcium carbonate concentration, and is expressed as milligrams of calcium carbonate per liter of water (mg/l $CaCO_3$) or in a dH number.

For general community aquariums, hardness is rarely an issue. Rift Lake cichlids such as the Malawi cichlids require hard water, like their native lakes. Many community tropical fish originate in areas of soft water, but many of them have been bred in captivity for so many generations that they are able to thrive in a wide variety of water hardness.

As a general guide, soft water is 0—100 mg/l $CaCO_3$ (0—5.5 dH); above this would be classed as hard, with very hard water at 300+ mg/l $CaCO_3$ (18+ dH).

Discus prefer low hardness, low pH water.

Carbonate hardness (kH)

Carbonate hardness is a measure of the bicarbonate levels in the water. If you boil hard water (which therefore has high carbonate hardness) the bicarbonate turns to carbonate. This is why it is called carbonate—and why you get lime-scale deposits inside your teakettle. kH is important because bicarbonate acts as a pH buffer, preventing or reducing pronounced pH swings. In well-stocked aquariums there is a tendency for the pH to gradually fall. This trend is opposed by the carbonate hardness. Once all of the bicarbonate is used up by this buffering action, a significant and dangerous drop in pH can occur. That is why we need to know about carbonate hardness.

Sources of carbonate hardness include regular water changes, calcium-based substrates and rocks, and commercially available buffering solutions. Carbonate hardness affects pH.

Ammonia, Nitrite, and Nitrate

Now we are getting to the core of good fish-keeping. Ammonia, nitrite, and nitrate are intricately linked with the nitrogen cycle.

Ammonia

Fish produce ammonia as part of their waste. This is excreted in urine and through the gills. Other sources of ammonia are decaying materials such as dead fish or uneaten food. Ammonia is present in two forms when dissolved in water—a relatively nontoxic ammonium form (NH_4+) and a much more toxic ammonia (NH^3). The proportion of ammonium NH_4+ to ammonia NH^3 depends on water temperature and pH. The higher both of these are, the more toxic NH^3 will be present.

Dwarf cichlids such
as the cockatoo dwarf
cichlids (Apistogramma
cacatuoides) are very
susceptible to elevated
dissolved ammonia
levels.

Points to remember about ammonia :

- Ammonia is removed primarily by the action of Ammonia Oxidizing Bacteria (AOB) present in your filters, which convert it to nitrite. In an emergency it can be removed by adding ammonia binding solutions (which actually covert the toxic NH^3 to non-toxic forms) or absorbing compounds such as zeolite, and can be reduced by partial water changes.

- Persistent ammonia readings in an established aquarium suggest over-feeding, too many fish, or inadequate or faulty filtration.

- Sudden pH crashes may kill the AOB, causing a spike in ammonia levels.

- Ammonia-related water quality issues involve temperature, pH, and nitrite.

A school of neon tetras (Paracheirodon innesi) in a planted aquarium.

Nitrite

Ammonia is converted to nitrite by beneficial bacteria as part of the nitrogen cycle. Nitrite is much less toxic than ammonia, but is still very dangerous to your fish. Nitrite Oxidizing Bacteria (NOB) in your filter removes any nitrite present, converting it into nitrate.

Points to remember about nitrite:

- Persistent nitrite readings may be due to inadequate or faulty filtration.

- Low temperatures and very high ammonia concentrations mean the NOB in the filter is not working properly.

- Nitrite levels can be reduced by partial water changes. You can also add aquarium salt at a rate of 1 ounce (30 g) per 2.5 gallons (10 l). Do not use table or rock salt, as these can be toxic to fish; Even aquarium salt can be toxic to plants and some fish.

- Nitrite-related water quality issues are caused by ammonia and temperature.

Nitrate

Nitrate is produced by the action of NOB on nitrite. For most fish it is relatively nontoxic, but some are more sensitive to it than others; high levels can stress the fish, making them more susceptible to disease. Some invertebrates, such as shrimps, can have molting difficulties, if exposed to high nitrate concentrations.

- Nitrate-related water quality issues are caused by ammonia and nitrite.

All goldfish, including this Moor, place much more load on biological filters than smaller, tropical fish.

Nitrogen Cycle

The constant removal of ammonia and nitrite from your aquarium water by using AOB and NOB bacteria is known as biological filtration. The reactions involved form part of the nitrogen cycle, and as a fishkeeper you should be familiar with how this works. As outlined previously, the problem with ammonia is that it is very toxic to fish. In the wild, fish are usually found in such large volumes of water that this ammonia is immediately diluted, but in the confines of your aquarium the ammonia builds up. This is why we need biological filtration.

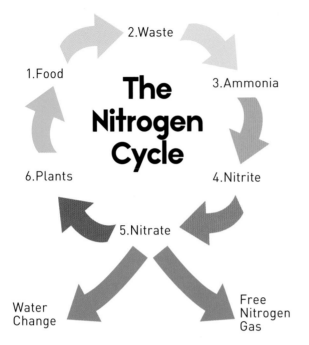

The Nitrogen Cycle

1. Food
2. Waste
3. Ammonia
4. Nitrite
5. Nitrate
6. Plants

Water Change

Free Nitrogen Gas

Biological filters provide a suitable environment for the beneficial (AOB) bacteria that are known collectively as nitrosomonas to grow. These AOB feed on dissolved ammonia and convert it into a less toxic compound, nitrite.

Nitrite is still toxic, but another group of bacteria come to the rescue. Collectively referred to as nitrobacter, these NOBs convert any nitrite into nitrate.

Nitrate is considerably less toxic than nitrite and many fish can tolerate high levels, although invertebrates such as shrimps may be less forgiving.

Nitrate is a problem, however. In an ideal nitrogen cycle, nitrate would:

1. Be absorbed by plants as food, converted into plant tissue, which, if then eaten by a fish, would complete the nitrogen cycle.

2. Be broken down by bacterial degradation in areas of low oxygen (anaerobic) into free nitrogen gas (denitrification).

3. Be converted back to ammonia (again completing the cycle).

The problem is that this does not happen in most aquariums, and if we do nothing nitrate levels can become extremely high over time. This can usually be traced to:

• Too many fish causing the production of significant levels of nitrate.

• Not enough live and healthy plants relative to the fish population to utilize much of the nitrate produced.

- No anaerobic areas that allow for denitrification to occur are present.

In these situations, you can control the nitrate level with partial water changes (although you must make sure the nitrate levels in your tap water or other water source are lower than in your aquarium) or by using nitrate-removing chemical filtration products.

Oxygen

Fish rely on oxygen dissolved in their water to breathe. Water has less oxygen than air, and warm water holds less oxygen than cold water. Almost all of the oxygen in a body of water gets there by dissolving into it at the surface. The more agitated the surface, the more oxygen can dissolve. This is why filter outlets placed right at the surface, or spray bars just above it, are so popular. They disturb the surface and enhance oxygenation. Even air stones, air curtains, and air-powered ornaments work this way, by bringing less oxygenated water from lower in the aquarium up to the surface. Bubbles also create new surface when they burst at the top, but provide hardly any direct oxygenation at typical aquarium depths.

In a well-stocked aquarium, a bubbling air stone creates a focal point as well as much-needed water circulation.

Always make sure that the water surface is rippling or in motion. Powerheads and internal filters placed well below the surface will circulate water, but, if the surface is still, oxygen levels can become dangerously low. Fish that are suffering from oxygen starvation will gasp at the surface. Remember that it is not just your fish that need oxygen—your plants and filter bacteria need it too.

Large fish such as this black angelfish (Pterophyllum scalare) are more susceptible to low dissolved oxygen levels.

Carbon dioxide

Carbon dioxide is a byproduct of normal respiration. In the aquarium it is produced by your fish, plants and largely by your filter bacteria. It is acidic and high levels can cause a fall in pH, but luckily it comes out of the water and into the air at the surface very easily, so normal water circulation will prevent problems.

Chlorine

Many water companies add chlorine, or chloramine, to their water supplies to reduce bacterial levels. These are toxic to fish, so whenever you do a water change you should use a proprietary dechlorinator.

Filters

Filters come in a variety of models. Most are driven by an electric powerhead. The smallest filters are usually internal filters and can consist of little more than a sponge cartridge through which water is drawn by a small powerhead. Larger internal filters are often designed to hold materials that provide physical, biological, and chemical filtration. Some aquariums come with built-in integral filtration units that are tucked unobtrusively in a back corner.

External filters follow the same general principle as internal ones, but because they are not constrained by aquarium size or viewing aesthetics, they can be quite large and contain several compartments that can be used for different types of filter **media**.

Internal filters (front) are typically smaller than external filters (rear).

External filters are usually housed kept the aquarium, often in a cupboard built into the design of the stand. Water is drawn down and pumped back into the aquarium through flexible tubing looped over the back. Their large size and ease of access for maintenance are major advantages over internal filters.

Sponge filters are sometimes used for smaller aquariums or breeding tanks. These are usually powered by air delivered by a pump rather than a powerhead. This gives a gentler flow that is safer for young fish.

Undergravel filters are somewhat less popular now. They are simple in structure and concept—an undergravel filter consists of a perforated plastic plate with one or two uplift tubes. It is installed during the set-up of the aquarium, beneath a layer of gravel some 2 inches (5 cm) deep. Air stones or powerheads are used to pull water along the uplifts, which then draws water down through the gravel. The gravel acts as both a physical filter and a biological medium. Undergravel filters are extremely effective biological filters, but need regular stirring and siphoning off of debris from within the gravel layers to prevent eventual clogging.

Excessive debris or disturbance by digging fish such as cichlids can cause interrupt water flows, which can dramatically reduce the functioning of the filter bed. Many plants do not seem to grow well in aquariums with undergravel filters. In an aquarium with just a few small, non-disruptive fish they can still work well.

Biological filter media will, over time, become progressively clogged with bacteria and debris, and so will need cleaning. But true cleaning, even under ordinary tap water, will remove the AOB and the NOB that you have worked so hard to establish. The best method is to rinse the filter in discarded aquarium water at the time of a water change, so that the bacteria left on the filter material will not be harmed. In larger aquariums two filters can be a better choice. Aside from doubling your filter capacity, it also means you can clean them alternately.

Aeration

For many of us, when we think about an aquarium, we picture a stream of bubbles rising to the surface somewhere. Air stones (porous rock that split an airstream into tiny bubbles) are an excellent way of giving good water circulation, although as we have mentioned, the bubbles actually do little oxygenation themselves.

Modern air pumps are much quieter than older models. Air curtains can produce dramatic effects with enhanced circulation.

Once air pumps were essential and all filters were air-powered, but now much of the equipment is run with electric motors. However, air stones can still have their place. They can enhance oxygenation by keeping the water circulating and churning at the surface. Air curtains produce a more dramatic effect across the entire tank.

Test Kits

Test kits are vital pieces of equipment. Without them you have no idea of what is really happening in your aquarium. Most of the commonly available test kits are colorometric—you interpret the result by comparing a color change to a chart provided. Types of testing kits include:

Dip strips

These are strips with small squares that are pretreated with chemicals. They are dipped into your aquarium water and the results compared to a chart at specific time intervals. Often several tests are incorporated on to one strip.

Liquid tests

Specific chemicals are added to a standard volume of water, and any color change is noted.

A color wheel to interpret pH tests.

Tablet tests

Similar to liquid tests, but the active ingredients are in tablets that have to be crushed or dissolved.

Electronic test kits

These are usually very accurate, if expensive.

A whole range of parameters can be tested, but the most important are ammonia, nitrite, and nitrate. Don't forget temperature as well!

Aquascaping

An aquarium can be thought of as a living work of art, and like any artwork, what you think is attractive is very subjective. Some aquarists look to mirror their fish's actual habitat and will research it thoroughly, while others will attempt artistic interpretations of landscape vistas by playing with scale, creating mountains from rocks and forests of dwarf plants. Other fishkeepers prefer bubbling divers, small castles, and sunken galleons. The truth is, as long as it does not harm the fish, anything goes.

I f we consider your aquarium as a canvas, looked at from the front, we can borrow some basic picture composition rules for aquascaping to create an attractive aquarium. If this seems a bit over the top, remember that a well-maintained aquarium could be the focal point of the room.

With a little planning, your aquarium can be a stunning, artistic mirror of nature.

Points to consider:

Asymmetry

Always try to avoid designing your aquarium layout too symmetrically. Such an aquarium loses its illusion of nature and much of its spontaneity.

The rule of thirds

Look at the front of your aquarium. Mentally (or on a piece of paper) draw two pairs of lines that will divide your aquarium into three sections vertically and three horizontally. You should aim to place your main objects of interest either along these lines, or where these lines cross. If you have a particular object, such as a plant, rock, or ornament that you wish to use as a **focal point**, place it as best you can where two of these lines intersect.

Plants and rocks can be used as focal points.

The rule of odds

The human brain automatically tries to make sense of any scene it sees, and one thing it does is to look for symmetry. This it done by attempting to pair everything up. If you have even numbers of anything—plants, rocks, or bubbling divers—your brain will pair these up and this will lessen the impact of your display. Therefore, try to keep odd numbers of plants, rocks and aquarium ornaments, so that the brain cannot form pairs. This will give you more of a feeling of the randomness that is found in nature.

Bigger things go to the back

Generally, taller plants, rocks and driftwood are placed towards the back, while smaller objects or plant life are brought to the front. This helps to give an illusion of depth.

Rock strata

Rocks strata (the lines or layers in rocks) in nature tend to run in the same direction, so if you are trying to reproduce a rock formation effect, try to use similar-looking rocks and have them all roughly arranged at a similar angle. Only use rocks bought at your aquarium supply store. Rocks from unknown sources may contain toxic minerals.

Substrate size

For natural-looking aquarium use different size substrates at different places in the tank. For example, use aquarium sand, then small gravel with some larger pebbles and rocks scattered on to it to resemble a river bed. Make sure that there is not too much variation in the colors or tones.

Artificial rocks and caves can be just as good as the real thing—just ask this angelfish.

Proportion

Try to keep everything in proportion. If you are trying to suggest a mountain range with a series of large rocks, keep small fish. Big fish with small castles just look wrong!

Driftwood

This and similar woods can add a strong natural element to an aquarium, often helping to form the basic skeleton of your submerged work of art. Wooden roots and branches add visual interest, provide scaffolding for plants to grow on, resting places for certain fish, and help define territorial boundaries for others. Aquarium driftwood that has been naturally preserved with tannins. If it is dry then it is highly likely to float when placed in water—this is especially true for smaller pieces. Once it becomes waterlogged it will settle, but the tannins it contains will leach out into the water for quite a while. This is normal and should not be a cause for concern, as many of the fish we keep are native to tannin-stained waters. Activated carbon and partial water changes will progressively remove the tannins.

If you are really organized, you can place any new pieces into a bucket of water a week or so before you set up your aquarium, so that it becomes waterlogged. Otherwise, floating pieces of driftwood can be tied down to rocks or pieces of slate using cotton. Do not use driftwood from the beach as this will be saturated with salt that can be poisonous to your freshwater fish. Nor should you use fresh wood, as this may contain harmful substances in the sap. Feel free to experiment. After all, an aquarium is a personal thing.

Driftwood is used as a resting perch for a variety of fish, including this peckotlia catfish.

Aquarium Plants

Plants can add a lot to an aquarium, including aesthetic appeal, providing shelter and food for your fish, enhancing the water quality by converting fish waste products, and oxygenating the water. In reality, in the typical home aquarium, only the first two happen.

As for converting fish waste, not all plants will use nitrate as a food. Some will absorb ammonia instead, which can be good or it can interfere with the initial cycling of an aquarium. In an aquarium with a lot of fish, the nitrate produced may be more than what the plants need.

During the day, if there is enough light, plants convert light to energy (photosynthesis), and as a byproduct, they, release oxygen into the water (sometimes little streams of tiny bubbles can be seen trickling from leaves up towards the surface).

Mixing and matching
different artificial plants
can give a very realistic
display.

Dissolved carbon dioxide is used during photosynthesis and so, as this acidic substance is removed, the pH can rise. During the night photosynthesis stops, but the plants continue to breathe, using up oxygen, which means that they compete with the fish and the filter bacteria, and release carbon dioxide, which can cause a pH drop.

Another point to be aware of is that many aquarium plants are actually able to live both above and below the water. Such plants often have two forms—the immerse which grows beneath the surface, and an emerse, which grows above the surface. Some plants, such as Amazon swords (Echinodorus spp) are commercially grown in the emerse state; once placed into your fish tank the old emerse-form leaves will die off and be replaced by flimsier immerse ones.

True, beautiful, take-your-breath-away planted aquariums take a great deal of time and effort to achieve. In these set-ups the plants come first and are provided with lighting of the correct spectrum, fertilizer both in the substrate and dissolved in the water, carbon dioxide supplementation, and careful management of dissolved compounds such as phosphate.

To get a planted aquarium this good requires correct lighting, substrate, supplements and time.

Such aquariums also have just a few carefully selected fish that will not burrow or root too deep into the substrate, eat or damage the plants, or consume algae. Some of these aquariums are truly stunning, and it is possible to achieve this with research and effort. Many plants placed into normal community tank will fade and die because they are living organisms too, and just like fish, they have certain requirements. Those I would recommend when you're starting out include:

Java fern

Java fern (Microsorium pteropus) is robust and grows well in low light conditions. It can be trained to cling to rocks and driftwood, and can be bought already attached. Older leaves tend to turn brown and rot. It is slow growing, but extremely hardy, and is generally unpalatable to vegetarian fish. Suitable for tropical and temperate aquariums, it is available in at least two leaf forms.

Java moss

Java moss (Taxiphylluim barbieri) is another plant that does well at low light levels.

Pictured: Artificial plants don't need any special care and can be used with a variety of fish that are not plant-friendly.

Left to its own devices it will slowly spread into a mass of strands and will harbour all kinds of micro-organisms that your fish will love to graze on. Many fish will spawn on, or in it. Suitable for tropical or temperate aquaria, it can be grown or bought on driftwood or rocks.

Amazon swords

There are a variety of Amazon sword species and most are large. Planted singly in smaller tanks or in groups in larger aquariums, they usually do well under normal aquarium conditions. Expect the upright leaves to die off over a period of several weeks, to be replaced by similar, but less rigid, leaves. Amazon swords are tropical, but will tolerate temperatures up to 64° F (18° C).

Vallisneria

Vallisneria spiralis has long tape-like leaves that can be well over 12 inches (30 cm) long. Planted in groups, especially toward the back, these clumps will thicken as the parent plants send out runners across the surface of the substrate. It thrives in both tropical and temperate conditions.

Anubias

These African plants have broad, flat leaves and are very tolerant of low light levels. In fact, if exposed to too much illumination, they can suffer badly from algae overgrowth. They generally grow very slowly, and, like the Java fern and moss, can be grown on rocks an driftwood. This is suitable for tropical aquariums only.

Canadian pond weed

Canadian pond weed (Elodea canadensis), typically sold in bunches, can grow very rapidly and will quickly become quite straggly without appropriate lighting and pruning. The rapid growth means that it competes with nuisance algae for available dissolved nutrients, and many fish will eat it, so it can be a good source of greens and fiber. It is suitable for temperate tanks only. Be careful where you dispose of this plant, as it can quickly become a pest in native waterways. This, and the related species E. densa, are illegal in some U.S. states.

Two of the remaining functions of plants—aesthetics and shelter—can be achieved just as well with artificial plants. There are some very realistic plastic, acrylic, and silk plants available today. These can be mixed and matched for form, color, texture, and size to give some truly remarkable results. You can even combine them with real plants too. If artificial plants become algae-coated they are easily removed, cleaned off with a mildly abrasive pad, and replaced. They can also be kept with plant-eating fish such as silver dollars (Metynnis spp) and will not succumb to the over-eager attentions of sucking catfish.

Plants are often considered an integral part of an aquarium, and it is true that some of the most stunning aquariums are heavily planted, but they are not essential. In fact many fish are found in waters where there are few or no plants.

Veiltail angelfish against a backdrop of plants growing on driftwood. Beautiful.

Setting up Your Aquarium

This is the beginning of the exciting part—setting up your aquarium. All the reading and thinking that you have been doing on filtration systems, water quality, and what fish you are going to keep is now becoming real.

The steps to setting up a successful aquarium:

1. Place your aquarium on a dedicated stand or on furniture strong enough to hold the total weight. All-glass aquariums, especially medium to large ones, are best set on a soft, conforming base. This is to even out any minute differences in pressure between the aquarium stand and the glass base that could cause cracks when the tank is filled. Foam bases are available, or as an alternative use ceiling tiles cut to size. Avoid direct sunlight.

2. Add any large rocks or other heavy ornaments. Then add your gravel or other substrate, and press other ornamentation, such as driftwood, into place. If you are using an undergravel filter this will need to be positioned first.

3. Begin adding water. Siphon or gently pour water on to a small plate placed on the gravel, allowing the water to spill over the side so you are less likely to disturb your initial aquascaping.

Setting up your aquarium.

4. The water that you are adding at this stage need not be heated, but should contain a water conditioner to remove any chlorine and heavy metals that may be present in your tap water. Bubbles will form on the sides of the aquarium and on the surfaces within— this is normal. If the aquarium is not too deep— between 12 and 18 inches (30 and 45 cm)—then wait until the aquarium is 80% full before adding any more aquascape elements, as you can best judge what the effect will be in at this point. For a deeper aquarium, wait until it is around one-third full. Some people will add live plants at this stage. If you are going to do this, fill with water warmed to the correct temperature, as many plants will not tolerate a cold shock.

5. Once the tank is around 80% full, install the heater and internal filters, or the siphons, return pipes, and spray bars for external filtration units. Switch on and prime your filters, making sure everything is working well. It is common filters to have air pockets when they are first run. These can make the filtration unit seem noisy and may cause intermittent fine sprays of tiny bubbles into the aquarium. Once these are going steadily, you can begin to add the tank maturation product according to the instructions—you have started cycling your aquarium (see page 90).

6. Switch on the power to your heaters once the aquarium is full.

7. Put the cover or the lid in place.

8. Now leave your aquarium to settle in for a few days. Check the temperature frequently to make sure that it is reaching your desired temperature (or room temperature, if you have a temperate aquarium). Live plants benefit from at least five to seven days to start to establish themselves before introducing any fish. If live plants are used, start switching the light on (or put on a timer), as they need to start to photosynthesize.

A slice of the Amazon—discus (Symphysodon sp) combined with rummy-nosed tetras (Hemigrammus rhodostomus).

Cycling Your Aquarium

Cycling an aquarium is the process of establishing and maturing the biological filtration necessary for the safe and rapid conversion of ammonia into nitrate. Failure to cycle your aquarium will result in New Tank Syndrome, and will cause unnecessary suffering to your fish.

New Tank Syndrome happens when fish are added to a new aquarium immediately after it is set up. With no added filter maturation products, high numbers of fish and regular feeding, the ammonia levels rapidly rise to 2.0 mg/l and above, causing fatalities in all but the hardiest of fish.

Cycling an aquarium typically takes some three to four weeks, but it can take longer, because each aquarium is different.

Once you are happy that your aquarium is settling down, the temperature is stable, and all pumps and filters are working, start adding your maturation product. Such products contain colonies of the beneficial AOB and NOB that you need in your filtration system to make your aquarium suitable for keeping fish. Bacteria can be added as:

• Commercial products. The bacteria are present either in a liquid suspension, gel, or powder.

• Seeding from an established filter by transferring some filter materials.

• Introducing live plants will bring in some beneficial bacteria—if they have been grown submersed in an established aquarium.

To establish a population of filter bacteria you need a source of ammonia. Usually this is the fish, but there are fishless methods of cycling an aquarium, using either pure ammonium added directly to the aquarium or allowing something high in protein to rot in your tank—sometimes a piece of shrimp is used. These methods, although arguably better from a fish welfare point of view, are less predictable. Most aquarists use a combination of good commercial bacterial supplement, combined with the introduction of small numbers of ammonia-tolerant fish.

No fish is immune to ammonia, however, and even those suggested here should be closely monitored for signs of ill health.

Commonly available species of fish that are suitable for the initial cycling of an aquarium are:

- **Danios**, especially the zebra danio (Danio rerio) and all of its forms, plus the pearl danio (D. albolineatus). Both suitable for tropical or temperate aquariums.

- **White cloud mountain minnows** (Tanichthys albonubes). They are suitable for tropical or temperate aquariums.

- **Corydoras catfish** (Corydoras sp) for tropical tanks, and the peppered catfish (normal and albino) is suitable for temperate aquariums.

- **Barbs (Barbus sp)** can be quite big and boisterous as adults, and should only be bought if you are confident that they will fit into the final community you are planning.

- **Tetras** such as the neon tetra (Paracheirodon innesi) and cardinal tetra (P. axelrodi) are suitable for tropical or temperate aquariums.

Neon tetras, initially in very small numbers, can be used for cycling a tropical aquarium.

Cycling your aquarium is really where your test kits and notebook come in, because you need to keep a record of the different water quality readings over the days to help you judge how your aquarium is maturing. Your essential test kit should cover pH, ammonia, nitrite and temperature.

How to cycle your aquarium

- Most bacteria supplied in the maturation products are present in a dormant form, and can take between two to six days to become active. When all the equipment is running smoothly in your aquarium, start adding the maturation product according to the instructions on the package.

- After a few days it will be safe to add some fish. Only buy a small number—around two or three, depending on the size of the fish and the tank.. Feed very small amounts several times daily. Check the ammonia level and make a note of it in your notebook. This is day one of cycling.

- Every day, check the ammonia level and note it. It should progressively climb and reach a peak around day 10 to 14. Once the ammonia reaches a level of around 2.0 mg/l, start monitoring your fish very closely. Continue to add maturation product and, if this does not halt the rise, add an 'ammonia-locking' solution.

A fully cycled and fully stocked tropical aquarium.

These products convert ammonia into less toxic ammonium—your test kit will measure and read the total ammonia (the sum of NH_3 and NH_4+). The filter bacteria will still be able to work on the ammonium to convert it to nitrite, but it will be less toxic to your fish. The peak ammonia concentration is likely to be high—up to 4.0 or 5.0 mg/l. Once the AOB numbers in your filtration system have multiplied to a level where they can remove all of the ammonia present, you will see a sudden and dramatic fall in ammonia. This can occur literally within 24 hours. It can seem a long time coming, but is exciting when it happens, and means you're half way there.

• Around day five to seven, start to measure nitrite levels. Initially this can be done every other day. The same process that the AOB went through, your NOB now have to go through. At this point there will be a huge population of AOB kicking out vast amounts of nitrites for a relatively small population of NOB to deal with. Now the NOB, with all this nitrite available, begins to multiply. This process always seems to take longer than the first part—nitrites typically peak around day 25 to 35, but even after levels have fallen, there is often nitrite present for several weeks.

• Now nitrates will begin to rise, and their levels are kept in check largely by partial water changes.

- Once the nitrite peak has come and gone, you can add more fish. Aim to stock over a period of three to four months or more. Each time you add a new fish, the bacterial populations need to go through the same process of multiplying to meet demand. Therefore, after each addition monitor your ammonium and nitrite levels closely. Demand is relative, however. If you have one fish and add a second identical fish, you have doubled the ammonia load on your filter system. On the other hand, if you have 10 fish and you add one more identical one, then you have increased the load only by about 10%.

- In a mature tank, but your filtration system should be healthy enough to respond quickly to variations in fish load.

- Check your pH at least every two to three days. The high levels of bacteria that you are encouraging can cause an inadvertent fall in pH.

- Cycling an aquarium can take up to five weeks, because every tank is different. This is not wasted time, however; you are preparing the tank for the aquarium that you first visualized in your head. This time will give you valuable experience looking after those first few fish needed to cycle your aquarium, and a chance to research species you wish to keep once those nitrite levels fall. There are probably 200 species of fish commonly available in aquarium stores, that are suitable for a community tank, and even more once you begin to look at special-ist set-ups or less common species. Take the time while your aquarium is maturing to read, research, and talk to the staff in your local aquarium supply. Impulse buys often end up as problems.

Take time to add all the fish you want. Give your tank time to handle the load.

Populating Your Aquarium

Remember at the beginning of the book we said that setting up an aquarium is a marathon and not a sprint? Well, the finish line is in sight. Your aquarium is cycled and you have a few, small, nonaggressive fish looking very lost in the tank. Do you rush out and buy a whole load of fish right away? As you might have guessed, the answer is no.

Aside from researching individual fish species, you need to consider how many fish your aquarium can support. As a general rule, 1 inch of fish to about 12 square inches (2.5 cm to 77 square cm) of surface area in a freshwater tropical tank (do not include the tail fin when measuring the fish). As an example, a 20-gallon (75 l) long tank measures 30 x 13 x 13 inches (76 x 33 x 33 cm) and has a surface area (the open area at the

Choosing the right fish for you

This dalamatian molly is a slim-bodied fish, and will need less surface area than a heavy-bodied goldfish.

top) of 390 square inches (the length times the width). Divide by 12 and you get about 33 inches of fish.

This is not a hard and fast rule, because you can stock fewer full-bodied fish or large fish in a tropical tank, and fewer still in a cold water tank. You'll find a handy tool to help you calculate how many fish you can stock in the Find Out More section (page 126).

Other factors that affect how many of what type of fish you can keep are:

1. Aquarium size. If your aquarium is 24 inches (60 cm) long, shoehorning a fish that grows to 18 inches (45 cm) into it is unfair and your fish will suffer.

2. Water quality. Filtration systems can be overloaded by excessively high fish populations. The aquarium will have poor water quality with very high nitrate levels and surges of ammonia and nitrite.

3. Low oxygen levels resulting from inadequate circulation can also be a problem. More advanced forms of filtration can potentially enable you to stock more fish, but at the risk of a catastrophe if you suffer a prolonged power cut, for example.

4. Sociability. Some fish are natural loners. They may be territorial either permanently, or just while breeding, and attempt to defend an area of the aquarium, sometimes to the death. Their behavior in the confines of an aquarium may be different from that in the wild. Midas cichlids (Amphilophus citrinellum) will form schools in the wild when not spawning; in aquariums, it can be difficult to keep individuals together in all but the largest tanks.

5. Do not judge your potential fish numbers by what you see in the aquarium stores. These fish are usually kept in large systems where all of the

aquariums are connected, plus there will be high-tech filtration equipment so that in reality these fish are swimming in a huge volume of water.

6. The biological load of invertebrates is considered tiny and any shrimps, snails, and so on that you are thinking of stocking can normally be exempt from your calculations, unless their numbers are going to be large.

Goldfish (here a calico ryukin and red and white bubble-eye) are large, messy fish that require a relatively large amount of space.

Other guidelines to consider when choosing fish are:

Less is more

Schooling fish always look better in larger numbers of the same species. The various tetras, for example, will school together. If you are planning on buying schooling fish, always buy at least five or more. Fish will school primarily as an anti-predator behavior. The more fish they swim with, the less chance they have of being selected by a predator. Schooling fish in a group are happy; a single fish is nervous and stressed. Keeping such fish in larger groups makes them more confident, which means that they are more likely to display normal behavior. A group of male black phantom tetras (Megalamphodus megalopterus) with their jet black sail-like dorsal fins erect, or the vibrant colors of displaying boesemani rainbowfish (Melanotaenia boesemani) are a sight to behold. Many aquarium stores offer discounts if you buy several of the same species of schooling fish. You can have a stunning aquarium with schools of just one or two species of fish.

Rule of odds

This is as true for groups of fish as it is for aquascaping. Where possible, buy odd numbers of schooling fish, as this looks more natural.

Water column

Some experts recommend selecting fish based on the level in the water column they are likely to swim, to give a balanced appearance. But, unless your aquarium is exceptionally deep, this is unlikely to work. Substrate dwellers such as Corydoras catfish will spend most of their time on the bottom, but will swim to the surface to gulp air and to take food. Guppies (Poecilia reticulata) inhabit the top layers in nature, except that the top layer would be the first 12 inches (30 cm) or so of depth, which is the total depth of many tanks.

Janitors

Do not buy fish solely as janitors. Substrate feeders like corydoras are sometimes naively sold as "cleaners," along the lines of "they feed on any uneaten food." These fish do comb the bottom looking for food, but they will benefit from being kept in social groups (corydoras are a schooling species) and fed on sinking pellets and wafers. If they have to rely solely on leftovers they can slowly starve to death.

Healthy fish

Only select from healthy-looking fish. Look at the other fish in the same tank. If there are any obviously sick ones, do not buy any fish from that tank. For signs of a healthy fish, see Health.

Maintaining your aquarium

Now your aquarium is up and running and your first fish are at home, we move on the important part of keeping them at their best.

Water changes

Regular water changes are an essential part of fish-keeping. They help to reduce the level of organic compounds in the water and remove substances naturally found in water that can build up in your tank. . This can include trace elements such as iodine. A water change is literally your fishes' breath of fresh air.

It is better to change little and often, because then there is less variation in the make-up and quality of the water that the fish inhabit. Aim to change around 10% to 20% of the aquarium volume once a week. If you are only able to do this less often, then you can change more at a time.

Always use a dechlorinator with fresh water. In principle you should make sure the new water is at the same temperature as the aquarium, but in practice many fish seem to enjoy swimming in a bit cooler water for a few minutes.

Water changes can be used as an opportunity to clean your substrate, too. You can buy a gravel cleaner or vacuum—basically a siphon tube that you poke around in the gravel to suck up debris as you remove water. The pieces of gravel are disturbed and rolled around by the current generated by the siphon.

Siamese fighting fish (Betta splendens) are highly territorial towards other fighting fish and similar-looking species.

Feeding

Feeding most tropical and temperate community fish is fairly straightforward. There are several types of foods that are easy to get. These are:

Flakes and pellets

Most community fish will take commercial flake or pellet foods; there are a number of brands available and all are balanced nutritionally. There are also some specialist foods designed for particular groups of fish. For example, several companies offer "algal wafers" for loricarid catfish and other largely vegetarian fish, while others produce pellets just for Siamese fighting fish (Betta splendens).

Frozen foods

Frozen foods are arguably closer to the natural diet of many of the fish that we keep. The bulk of these frozen foods are invertebrates such as daphnia, bloodworm (Chironomus larvae), mosquito larva and brine shrimp. Freezing does not destroy certain disease-causing organisms such as mycobacteria, so those that have been irradiated are safest to feed your fish. Frozen foods can either be thawed out first before being fed, which enables the food to quickly disperse within the aquarium, or you can just drop a frozen block or part block into the water. As it melts, pieces of food will fall away, giving a more prolonged, although more local-ized, meal.

Frozen fish foods typically come in blister packets.

Live foods

Live foods trigger hunting behavior and can be an invaluable aid for inducing breeding. Brine shrimp, although nutritionally not ideal, are safe for freshwater fish because they are reared in salt water and will not transfer bacteria. Freshwater live foods, such as daphnia, tubifex worms, and bloodworm, may or may not come from cultured sources and so may pose a disease risk.

Feed your fish little and often. Most small fish are micro-predators and would normally feed opportunistically throughout the day on small invertebrates. We should attempt to mimic this by offering food at least twice a day, maybe up to four or five times, but only in small amounts. All food should be consumed around two to five minutes. If there is food left over then you are offering too much, and left over, uneaten food just puts extra strain on your filtration system. Many fish die from the effects that uneaten food has on their water quality, where it can cause fatal spikes of ammonia or nitrite.

Live bloodworm is taken eagerly by most fish.

Algae

Nuisance algae

Algae in your aquarium is inevitable. Algal spores are brought in on plants or fish and even blown in on drafts. Usually it is just an aesthetic problem, but occasionally it can get out of hand. A surge of algal growth is normal in newly established aquariums, as nutrient levels can be high and competing live plants are neither established nor numerous enough to grab any dissolved nutrients. In more mature aquariums it is likely to be a management problem reflecting poor conditions. Slime algae (Cyanobacterium, which is actually a type of bacteria) grows in blue-green sheets that expand during the day and contract at night. This is typical of high nutrient, poor water quality conditions.

Physical removal

There are an assortment of mildly abrasive scrubbing pads and magnetic algae cleaners available in stores.

These can be good at removing all or most of the algae from off the glass sides of the aquarium; if you have an acrylic aquarium only use the cleaning tools recommended, because some scourers will scratch acrylic. Slime algae can be siphoned off the substrate and ornaments.

Magnetic algae scrubbers make glass cleaning easy. Take care you don't get substrate caught in it!

Nutrient control

High fish densities predispose to high algal growth by providing lots of food for the algae, usually as high nitrate levels (due to over stocking) and high phosphate levels (from fish food). Partial water changes, nitrate and phosphate absorbers, and reducing fish numbers will help.

Lighting

The light spectrum or intensity may be wrong for live plants, so they grow poorly and are out-competed by algae. Reducing the hours the lights are on, or changing or upgrading your lighting system, may help.

Keeping algae eaters

Only choose these if you want them to be a part of your aquatic community. All of these are animals with specific needs that need to be met—they are not merely small fishy vacuum cleaners. None of these fish will touch slime algae.

Sucking loach

Sucking loach (Gyrinocheilus aymoneri) are cute when small, but they can grow up to be 11 inches (27 cm) long, and aggressive, too. Probably not recommended long term for a normal community aquarium. Normally they come in shades of brown, but a yellow or gold version is available.

Siamese algae eater

Siamese algae eater (Crossocheilus siamensis) grows up to 6 inches (15 cm) and eats a wide variety of algae, but is not very colorful.

Ancistrus catfish

These sucking catfish are excellent for algal control. They do not grow too big (between 4 and 6 inches—10 and 15 cm). They may **spawn** in a community aquarium, where the male will dig or take over a burrow and tend the eggs and newly hatched fry. Usually colored in browns and grays, a stunning golden albino morph is occasionally available, as is a long-finned variety.

Peckoltia sabaji is an omnivore that needs some meaty food in its diet. Grows up to 10 inches (25 cm).

Otocinclus catfish

A small (2 inches—5 cm) sucking catfish that prefers to be in schools and can be delicate.

Other sucking catfish

Generally, for algae control, these are a mixed bunch. Some are good but just grow too big, such as the sailfin pleco (Pterygoplichthys gibbiceps) at 20 to 24 inches (50 to 60 cm), while others are not vegetarian.

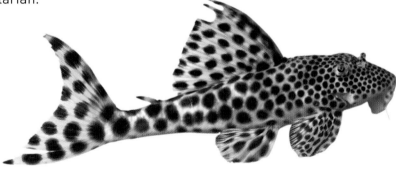

Algae-eating shrimp

Algae-eating shrimp or amano shrimp (Caridina japonica) are small, semi-transparent shrimp that are hardy and suitable for tropical or temperate aquariums. If kept in reasonable numbers they can collectively do a very good job of keeping algae under control.

Chemical control

There are a variety of products that can be added to the aquarium to kill algae. I would suggest these as a last resort. They may give temporary improvement, but you are better off trying to address any underlying factors, such as poor water quality.

The algae-eating shrimp is ideal for tanks with small fish or nanoaquariums.

Routine Aquarium Care

The routine chores that will keep your aquarium in top condition do not take a lot of time—especially if you do them regularly. Check the maintenance instructions that came with your filter, because they may be different from those given here.

Tips for routine aquarium care

Daily

- Feed your fish.

- Check temperature.

- Check filtration systems are working.

Cute, but this baby oscar (Astronotus occellatus) will grow to a foot (30 cm) with an appetite to match!

Weekly

- Do water quality tests and log them.

- Partial water change.

- Remove algae from aquarium glass.

- Clean sponge filters.

Monthly

- Clean artificial plants and ornaments.

- Clean or change component parts on filters, according to manufacturer's instructions.

Six months to one year

- Change lighting tubes.

Signs of Health

- Healthy fish will usually be alert and responsive to what is going on around them.

- Their swimming pattern will be normal.

- The fins are usually at half-mast or fully erect.

- The color will be normal and the skin surfaces un-blemished.

- Breathing will be largely unnoticeable, but of slow to moderate rate.

- They will eat readily if offered appropriate food.

Erect fins, bright colors and balanced position denote a healthy Columbian tetra (Hyphessobrycvon equadoriensis).

Signs of Illness

- Fish are listless and fins are clamped.

- Some fish may persistently rub or scratch against the substrate or ornaments.

- Breathing may be rapid or exaggerated. Fish may appear to gasp at the surface.

- Swimming movements are abnormal for that species. The fish may be unable to keep an even keel; very weak fish just drift with the current, or become drawn on to or stuck to filter inlets.

- Colors may be dulled; gray patches of mucus may be obvious.

- There may be obvious skin abnormalities, including white spots, fluffy cottonlike patches, and red ulcers.

Avoid mollies with clamped fins that shimmy in one spot.

Just like us, fish can suffer from a wide range of ailments. Some of these are easy to sort out, some are difficult and some almost impossible. You will see a range of off-the-shelf treatments available in your local aquarium store, but these have varying levels of effectiveness. Fish antibiotics may also available off the shelf.

How to look for signs of Illness in your fish

These products are generally safe to use in your aquarium. Some species or types of fish can be sensitive to certain ingredients; for example, Do not use products with copper or formalin with scaleless fish such as the clown loach (Botia macracantha) and black knife fish (Apteronotus albifrons). Usually there will be a warning on the label for any specific contraindications.

The key to getting the best out of these fish medicines is to be as accurate as possible with your diagnosis, but it is a truism that common things occur commonly. Some of the frequently encountered problems are listed on the next page. In the event of a disease outbreak always check your water quality, because this is often the source of the problem, and strive to maintain optimum conditions to give your fish their best chance of recovery.

White spot

White spot is caused by a single-celled parasite called Ichthyophthirius multifilis. It burrows into the skin where it grows, forming the characteristic white spot. It then drops off the fish, falls on to the substrate, and forms a protective cyst. In this stage the parasite divides into up to 200 new, free swimming forms that will swim off to find new fish hosts. White spot can be fatal if it severely damages the gills. Proprietary white spot medications are usually effective in dealing with the problem, especially combined with raising the temperature to around 82° F (28° C).However, recurrence is common.

Other skin parasites

Large parasites such as fish lice (Argulus sp) are occasionally encountered. These are easily visible with the naked eye and can be removed by first dabbing the louse with alcohol (which anesthetizes it and weakens its grip), and then removing it with a pair of tweezers. This is best left to a veterinarian.

Fish that are scratching, rubbing, have a high breathing rate, and/or patches of gray on the skin (excessive mucus production) are likely to have some microscopic parasitic problems. This can be one of several protozoal infestations or a fluke problem. Use a proprietary anti-protozoan medication.

Fungus

This classically looks like a cotton patch stuck on to the fish, which collapses when the fish is taken from the water. Proprietary medications including malachite green, 2-phenoxyethanol, or pimenta extract. Aquarium salt (not table salt) added to the water will often inhibit the growth of fungi. Many apparent fungal infections are actually parasitic, because the thick mucus that skin parasites trigger can form dense, fluffy patches on the skin surface.

Bacterial

Bacterial infections are common in ornamental fish. Typical symptoms include blood spots and ulcers. Some of these may respond to proprietary antibacterial medications. Some infections may require antibiotics.

Tumors

Fish, especially older ones, can develop tumors and growths. It can sometimes be possible for a veterinarian to operate and remove a growth, although this may depend upon a number of different factors including the size and location of the tumor.

Find Out More

Books

Boruchowitz, David E. *The Simple Guide to Freshwater Aquariums*. Neptune Beach, NJ: TFH Publications, 2001.

Jennings, Greg. *500 Freshwater Aquarium Fish: A Visual Reference to the Most Popular Species*. Toronto: Firefly Books, 2006.

Skomal, Gregory. *Freshwater Aquarium: Your Happy Healthy Pet*. New York: Howell Book House, 2005.

Web Sites

www.howmanyfish.com
How Many Fish? has simple tools to help you calculate how many fish your tank will support, the weight and volume of the tank, and how much gravel you need.

aquariuminfo.org
Aquarium Info has detailed guides for beginners on everything from calculating water volumes, to aquascaping to photographing your aquarium.

homeaquaria.com
Home Aquaria is an information hub, bringing together home aquarium enthusiasts from all over the world.

 **Words to Understand**

algae a simple, single-celled plant

aquascape arrange all the elements in an aquarium to make an appealing overall design

focal point the center area of interest

invertebrate an animal that lacks a backbone, such as shrimp

media in aquariums, the substance used for filtration in a filter

school a large group of animals that stay together in the water

siphoning the act of using a tube to draw liquid upwards

spawn releasing eggs to reproduce

substrate the bottom layer of sand or gravel in an aquarium

temperate a cooler temperature; about 64° to 72° F (18° to 22° C) in an aquarium

tropical a warmer temperature, as in the tropics; about 72° to 80° F (22° to 26° C) in an aquarium

Index